# A STEP-BY-STEP BOOK ABOUT
# RABBITS

## ANMARIE BARRIE

**Photography**
Bruce Crook; Marvin Cummings; Michael Gilroy; H. Hanson; Burkhard Kahl; Louise B. Van der Meid; Mervin F. Roberts; Robinson; Vince Serbin.
**Humorous illustrations by Andrew Prendimano.**

**1995 Edition**

9 8 7 6 5 4 3 2 1                                                   9  6 7 8 9

Distributed in the UNITED STATES to the Pet Trade by T.F.H. Publications, Inc., One T.F.H. Plaza, Neptune City, NJ 07753; distributed in the UNITED STATES to the Bookstore and Library Trade by National Book Network, Inc. 4720 Boston Way, Lanham MD 20706; in CANADA to the Pet Trade by H & L Pet Supplies Inc., 27 Kingston Crescent, Kitchener, Ontario N2B 2T6; Rolf C. Hagen Ltd., 3225 Sartelon Street, Montreal 382 Quebec; in CANADA to the Book Trade by Vanwell Publishing Ltd., 1 Northrup Crescent, St. Catharines, Ontario L2M 6P5 ; in ENGLAND by T.F.H. Publications, PO Box 15, Waterlooville PO7 6BQ; in AUSTRALIA AND THE SOUTH PACIFIC by T.F.H. (Australia), Pty. Ltd., Box 149, Brookvale 2100 N.S.W., Australia; in NEW ZEALAND by Brooklands Aquarium Ltd. 5 McGiven Drive, New Plymouth, RD1 New Zealand; in Japan by T.F.H. Publications, Japan—Jiro Tsuda, 10-12-3 Ohjidai, Sakura, Chiba 285, Japan; in SOUTH AFRICA by Lopis (Pty) Ltd., P.O. Box 39127, Booysens, 2016, Johannesburg, South Africa. Published by T.F.H. Publications, Inc.
MANUFACTURED IN THE UNITED STATES OF AMERICA
BY T.F.H. PUBLICATIONS, INC.

# CONTENTS

# INTRODUCTION

Rabbits have been in existence for at least three and a half million years. Their footprints have been found in fossilized rock in Africa. Early rabbits were natives of the lands bordering the western Mediterranean Sea, and they were first domesticated about 4000 years ago.

Being mammals, rabbits nourish their liveborn young with milk, are in the main covered with hair, have a four-chambered heart and are warm-blooded. Although there are about twenty-five species of rabbits, only one has been domesticated: *Oryctolagus cuniculus.* Like rodents, rabbits have incisors that grow constantly and must be worn down. However, rabbits are not rodents. Though at one time they were considered to be rodents, for many years now taxonomists have thought them to be sufficiently different from rodents to have their own order, the order Lagomorpha.

Rabbits are also quite different from hares. Rabbits are born blind, deaf and naked in underground burrows. In contrast, hares are born already furred in a nest of grass, with some vision, hearing and a better ability to get around. Hares are also wild and undomesticated.

It is estimated that about 12 million rabbits are raised in the United States each year, and that number is increasing. England, Germany, France and Spain produce even more rabbits than the U.S. Rabbits are also becoming more popular in China, South and Central America and Africa.

Rabbits' capacity to multiply makes them easy to breed and raise. This high fertility rate results from the fact that a female rabbit does not have a specific period during which she is receptive to mating. Instead, a doe will allow copulation with a buck, and then, a few hours later, she will ovulate. In a

FACING PAGE:
One reason that rabbits are popular as pets is that
they're cute and cuddly—but there are other reasons
as well.

A lop rabbit sniffing flowers. Rabbits are vegetarians, but they shouldn't be allowed to eat heavily of wild plants.

month she will give birth to the young. Six to eight weeks later the babies are weaned. With this timetable, a doe can produce five or even six litters of six to eight young per year during the three most fertile years of her life. It is estimated that a single pair of rabbits and their progeny can produce around 13 million rabbits in that time!

Rabbits are kept and raised for a variety of reasons. Many are domestic pets; others are used to produce serums, hormones, and antitoxins in testing laboratories. There are those rabbits bred in order to be exhibited in shows for color, pattern, shape, size and other features. Primarily, though, rabbits are bred for their nutritious meat. Some breeds may produce meat more efficiently than others, but all domestic rabbits are edible and taste about the same. Their meat costs about the same as chicken. A pound of rabbit meat can be generated from less than three pounds of dry vegetable pellets. A chicken uses no less an amount of grain, but the grain is more expensive.

# Introduction

Additionally, use is made of rabbit fur. Arctic fur, clipped seal and polar seal are some of the names for rabbit fur. Used to adorn collars and cuffs and to make whole coats, rabbit pelts are replacing more traditional furs. Real felt is actually made from rabbit fur. Some varieties of rabbit, like the Angora, produce up to twelve ounces of rabbit wool per year. These animals are simply sheared; they do not have to be killed.

Rabbit droppings are a great fertilizer for flowers, vegetables, trees and shrubs. The manure may be applied without aging, with or without lime, because it will not "burn" plants, as will other fertilizers. Rabbit droppings have a higher fertilizer value compared to other farm manures. In addition, earthworms, used for fishing bait, can be raised in the droppings. When the worms are removed, the manure remaining is still a desirable fertilizer for gardens and plants.

These lop rabbits have been allowed to roam outside on a nice sunny day, but they should not be left unsupervised.

# RABBITS AS PETS

Rabbits do wonderfully well in captivity. They are easy to breed and very hardy animals. Rabbits do not readily acquire diseases from humans, nor are they likely to transmit them. Cages are inexpensive to buy or simple to construct yourself. Of course, rabbits are not often kept indoors, but on a rare occasion a pet has been housebroken. And their small, hard droppings are not really objectionable.

Rabbits require a simple diet of rabbit pellets, supplemented with occasional tidbits of bread and vegetables. The pellets are not expensive and are available in most pet shops. Stale bread can be obtained from your local baker, and vegetable tops and clippings from your grocer, for little or no money. In fact, the baker and grocer will probably be happy to get rid of these unsalable items.

Rabbits are not comparable to a dog as companions. They cannot do the variety of tricks, nor are they as affectionate as a dog. However, they do not make noise and disturb the neighbors, and they can be kept in relatively small quarters where larger dogs are prohibited. Rabbits do respond to your attention. They like to be picked up and handled. Your rabbit will be glad to see you and can show some affection. It can even be taught a few simple tricks.

Being kept in an cage, they are easily controlled and not constantly under foot. And unlike cats, they won't scratch the furniture or eat the houseplants. Rabbits are very clean animals, bathing themselves much as cats do. Therefore, they do not require the grooming and bathing that can be a personal

FACING PAGE:
Large or small, rabbits have an undeniable appeal.
These are Netherland dwarf rabbits.

Lop rabbits have big ears—and provide big doses of pleasure.

FACING PAGE; upper photo: Brown is a common coat color in rabbits. Color has no effect on a pet rabbit's personality.

Children and rabbits can both have fun during play-time if someone watches them carefully.

FACING PAGE; lower photo: dwarf rabbits bred in Germany. Different countries recognize different breeds.

chore or a sizable expense if done by a professional.

Rabbits are probably best compared to hamsters, gerbils, chinchillas and guinea pigs as caged animals. Because most rabbits are larger, they lend themselves more to petting and handling. They also have a longer life expectancy, sometimes up to ten years or more. Yet they demand no more care than these smaller animals, and certainly much less attention than a dog or cat.

Rabbits need to be fed daily and their cages need regular cleaning. However, with the proper provisions, a rabbit can be left alone for a weekend. If you are planning an extended trip, though, you need to have a reliable person visit and care

for the rabbit every day. Fortunately, little maintenance is involved.

Rabbits are easily transported in a cage. Therefore, they can be taken to another house for care, or they will even enjoy accompanying you on your trip!

The rabbit breeders recognize at least forty distinct breeds of rabbits. Distinguished by different colors or patterns within these breeds are several varieties. Many types were first developed for a specific purpose, such as meat or fur production. Others were bred for exhibition or just for suitability as pets. The following are among the most popular breeds:

# BREEDS AND VARIETIES

## American

Adults weigh eleven pounds. They come in white and a solid, dark, clear slate-blue. This breed originated in the United States.

## Angora-English

This breed has been known since 1765 and most likely originated in Ankara, Turkey. Adults weigh five and a half pounds and they are raised for their coarse "wool." This coat requires more attention than normal rabbit fur and must be groomed at least once a month to keep the wool from becoming matted and tangled. The recognized colors are white, black, blue, and fawn.

## Angora-French

Adults are eight pounds and their wool is coarser than that of the English Angora. The colors are also white, black, blue, and fawn.

## Belgian Hare

Despite its name, this is actually a rabbit. The ideal weight is eight pounds and the body is large and lanky with long legs and ears. The fur is coarse and short, and the color is a shade of chestnut.

## Breeds and Varieties

### Beveren

This breed was developed in Belgium as a meat and pelt producer. The adults are ten pounds and are available in black, blue, brown, and a white variety with blue eyes.

### Blue Vienna

This breed is not common, but they make a good pet. Adults weigh nine and a half pounds and are, of course, blue.

### Brittania Petite

The color of this breed is white and the adults weigh two and a quarter pounds. They are not considered an ideal pet.

The Brittania petite is one of the smallest breeds; note the small ears typical of the dwarf breeds.

## Californian

This breed is always white with dark ears, nose, feet, and tail. Adults weigh nine and a half pounds and are popular for their meat and fur.

## Champagne D'Argent

Once known as the "French silver," the young are black and develop a typically silver color as they mature. Adults weigh ten and a half pounds, and they should look silvery, not yellow or brassy. This breed is raised for show and meat.

The dark ears and muzzle on this Californian rabbit nicely complement the white coat.

# Breeds and Varieties

Chinchilla rabbits are available in only one color, gray, but there are three size varieties.

## Checkered Giant

This is a large breed of rabbit weighing twelve pounds or more. They are white with black or blue spots checkered on the body. The placement of these patches is important for show animals. These animals are also raised for their fur.

## Chinchilla

There are three varieties of this breed: Standard, American, and Giant. The adult weights range from seven pounds for the standards up to fourteen pounds for the giant. All chinchillas are gray and raised for show and for fur. They have one of the finest coats of all rabbits, resembling a real chinchilla in both color and texture.

15

Rabbits are always on the alert during their waking hours, and they are very inquisitive about their surroundings.

Note the difference in expression between the young chinchilla rabbit above and the older specimen of the same breed below.

### Cinnamon

Adults weigh ten pounds and are rust or cinnamon in color. This breed is rare but makes a good pet.

### Creme D'Argent

These are cream colored rabbits weighing nine pounds, with orange and silvery highlights.

### Dutch

Weighing four and a half pounds, the Dutch pattern on the rabbits can be black, blue, chocolate, tortoise, steel gray, or gray. The uncolored part is always white. Dutch rabbits are good breeders, and the does are superior mothers. Excellent all-around pets, these animals are also raised for showing and for use in laboratories.

### English Spot

The ground color of this breed is white, with a chain pattern of black, gold, lilac, tortoise, gray, chocolate, or blue spots. These rabbits make excellent pets. They are also used for show, meat, and in laboratories. Adults weigh seven pounds.

Rabbits exhibiting the typical "Dutch-marked" pattern are available in a number of different colors.

Not often seen, the Havana rabbit has a beautiful plush coat.

### Flemish Giant

This is the largest of all the domestic rabbit breeds. Enthusiasts try to breed them to be as large and heavy as possible, fourteen pounds and over. The recognized color varieties are black, blue, fawn, light gray, sandy, steel gray, and white. These rabbits are raised primarily for show and meat.

### Florida White

This albino white is a relatively new breed. Adults average five pounds and make excellent pets.

### Harlequin

Once known as "Japanese," this breed was first exhibited in France in 1887. The fur is a patchwork of four distinct colors. The colors are black, blue, chocolate, and lilac, applied on a white background in the magpie variety and on an orange or dilute background in the harlequin variety. Adults of both varieties weigh eight pounds.

### Havana

Excellent pets, adults of this breed weigh five and a half pounds. The recognized colors are black, blue, and chocolate.

## Himalayan

Primarily show and meat rabbits, this breed is white with black or blue extremities and red eyes. The young are a silvery gray which whitens, and the nose, ears, feet, and tail darken. The colors tend to fade in older animals. Adults average three and a half pounds.

## Lilac

Adults weigh seven pounds and have lilac or pinkish gray fur. This breed is a good meat producer.

## Lops

The lop breeds include the Holland, English, French, and mini. Their outstanding feature is their extremely long, wide floppy ears which hang down the side of the head onto the floor. Two feet of ear spread is common. The typical color is fawn, but fawn and white, black and white, and tortoiseshell and white are known. The animals are used for show and in the laboratory and, depending on the variety, range from three to twelve pounds.

## Netherland Dwarf

The smallest of all rabbits, weighing only two pounds, this breed comes in twenty-one varieties. They are extremely

The color pattern of the Himalayan rabbit is similar to that of the Californian.

FACING PAGE:
Four female lop rabbits, each representing a different lop breed.

20

short-haired rabbits and come in almost every color and combination of colors available. They are popular pets and show rabbits.

## New Zealand

Adults weigh eleven pounds and come in white, brick-red, and black. Famous as a meat producer, this breed is also for showing and laboratory use.

## Palomino

Primarily a meat producer, this breed has a golden and a lynx variety. Adults weigh ten pounds.

## Polish

Small rabbits weighing two and a half pounds, the varieties are black, chocolate, blue-eyed white, and ruby-eyed white. Not an easy breeder, the principal uses are for show and laboratory.

Rex rabbits can make good pets, but they usually are kept for other reasons.

## Rex

Although raised primarily for its fur and for show, this breed is also a good producer of meat. The color varieties are black, blue, Californian, castor, chinchilla, chocolate, lilac, lynx, opal, red, sable, seal, and white. Adults, weighing nine pounds, can be solid or a mixture of colors. The fur is plush, and its distinctive feature is that the guard hairs are the same length as the undercoat.

## Breeds and Varieties

**Rhinelander**
This breed weighs eight and a half pounds and has a white background with black and orange spots.

**Sable**
Weighing nine pounds, this breed is a rich sepia brown with purple on the head, feet, and ears.

**Satin**
This breed is recognized in black, blue, Californian, chinchilla, chocolate, copper, red, Siamese and white. The fur is unique because of its sheen; therefore its principal uses are for show and fur. Adults weigh ten pounds.

**Silver**
This breed comes in silvery shades of gray, fawn, and brown. Adults weigh six pounds and make excellent pets.

These sable rabbits have dark "points" on their ears and muzzles, making them Siamese sables.

**Silver Fox**

Formerly known as the "American Heavyweight Silver," this breed has long fur resembling that of a silver fox. The two color varieties are blue and black, and adults weigh ten and a half pounds.

**Silver Marten**

Primarily raised for showing and fur, this breed is black, blue, chocolate, or sable with silver-tipped guard hairs. Adults weigh eight and a half pounds.

**Tan**

Adults average four and a half pounds. The color varieties are black and tan, blue and tan, lilac and tan, and chocolate and tan.

Rabbits kept for show purposes must be groomed carefully before being exhibited.

**FUR TYPES**

Another way to classify rabbits is by fur type. Most of the breeds and varieties have normal fur, which is basically the same on any rabbit. It is about an inch long with a soft, fine, and dense undercoat.

**Rex** fur is found only on Rex rabbits. It is short and plush, being only five-eighths of an inch long. The guard hairs are the same length as the undercoat. Some people say the fur resembles velvet.

## Breeds and Varieties

Found only on rabbits in the satin breed, **satin** fur has a smaller diameter and is more transparent than normal fur. It is about an inch in length, but has more luster and more intense color than other furs.

The **Angora** breeds have fur that is referred to as wool. It is quite long, and one of the finest and softest coats imaginable. One animal can provide about twelve ounces of wool per year.

This orange rex rabbit shows the velvet-like fur typical of rex rabbits.

There are more than forty breeds of rabbits, ranging in size from two to twenty pounds, and some are particularly valuable for a specific characteristic. So you must decide what you want from your rabbit—a domestic pet, a provider of wool or fur, for meat, or for selective breeding.

# SELECTION

Regardless of its purpose, you should buy the best animal you can afford. A healthy rabbit is much easier to care for than one that is ill. And if you are choosing the animal for breeding purposes, it will take several generations to bring poor stock up to acceptable standards. The best way to improve any stock is to start with the best.

Visit a knowledgeable pet dealer or breeder, go to a rabbit show, and read books about rabbits. Do not buy the first animal that comes along. Rather, study several animals for comparison. Purchase a rabbit after you know what to look for; this might save you from making a mistake.

Fortunately, with few exceptions, all rabbits require the same treatment and respond similarly to care. However, you should know what type of rabbit you have so you can provide the proper size cage and the right amount of food. Remember that rabbits range in size from two to twenty pounds, so your feed bill could be much larger with a giant rabbit than with a dwarf. The larger animals are also more difficult to lift and carry around.

If you are interested in a rabbit for its meat, all specimens are edible, but some varieties, like the New Zealand, are better producers. They grow faster on less food. Angora rabbits provide enough wool for several pairs of gloves and yet still make good pets. Maybe you want a rabbit to show in competition? But as a pet, any rabbit is a good choice; even mongrels are as good as registered purebred rabbits. Of course, when

**FACING PAGE:**
Cradled safely in its owner's hands, this young rabbit feels secure.

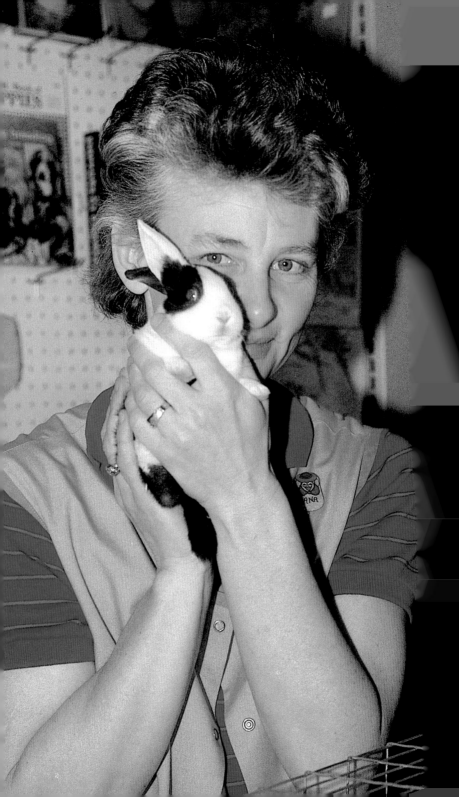

you select a crossbreed, you cannot be sure how large your pet may grow. Rabbits of different sizes will mate and the eventual size of their offspring cannot be determined.

Most likely you will choose a rabbit that is only two to three months old. Rabbits are usually weaned from their mother at around eight weeks of age. Up until that time, the babies need their mother's milk, or a specially prepared formula, to survive. Since a total of eight weeks with the mother is optimum for growth and development, do not accept a younger bunny.

Look for a rabbit that hops around and has an alert appearance. The eyes should be bright, not weepy. The nose should be clean and the insides of the forelegs should not be matted. If the fur is matted, it is a sign that the rabbit has a cold and has been wiping its nose with its front paws. Overall, the fur should be sleek and well groomed.

Avoid an animal with lumps, bumps, wounds, sores or bare spots. The front teeth should be even and unbroken, not overlapping or out of alignment. The vent area should be dry and clean. Any sign of dirt or stain indicates diarrhea. A healthy rabbit's droppings are hard and dry. Also check the toes and toenails. Even the rabbit's feet should be clean because well raised rabbits are brought up in cages with wire mesh floors that keep it out of its own excrement. The rabbit's ears need to be checked for crusty brown scales that signal ear mites.

Handle the rabbit in the store. It should feel well fed and fleshy, but not fat. Males tend to have better dispositions as pets than females, but the most important criterion in choosing your rabbit is its good health.

Pure white rabbits are big favorites.

FACING PAGE:
A healthy rabbit should *look* healthy; it should be interested in its surroundings and curious to explore new places.

# HOUSING

An important rule to remember when keeping rabbits is: one rabbit, one cage. It is not advisable to house two mature rabbits together because if they are both males they will fight, if they are both females they may fight, and if one is male and one is female they can mate without your blessing. Then you wind up with more rabbits than you had planned.

The size of the living quarters depends upon the size of your rabbit. So, before you buy or build an accommodation, know what type of rabbit you are going to buy. An adult rabbit should have one square foot per pound of live weight. Smaller varieties, like the dwarfs, need no less than four square feet of floor space no matter how tiny the animal. The height of the quarters is also important for keeping your pet comfortable. Eighteen inches is sufficient for dwarfs, increasing to as high as thirty inches for giants.

Rabbits need light, ventilation, protection from drafts and chills, and clean quarters. Hence, an all wire enclosure is the optimum choice for a rabbit home. They are inexpensive to buy and easy to build. Wire is easy to handle and will last for years, because a rabbit cannot chew through it and eat it. Unlike wood, wire will not become soaked and smelly with urine. In fact, an all wire floor permits droppings and urine to pass through to a box or tray that can be simply renewed and cleaned. Wire allows you to feed your pet conveniently, possibly without even opening a door.

A feed hopper and water bottle can be hung from the

Combined wood-and-wire hutch.

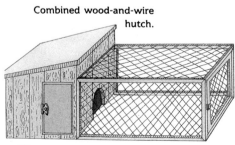

FACING PAGE:
Netherland dwarf rabbits of good quality.

outside of the cage, permitting you to fill them without disturbing your pet. Hanging them on the outside also means they will not take up any floor space in the cage. Through the wire, you can see your pet at all times. Yet, you can reach in and pick up the rabbit when you desire.

A rectangular mesh approximately five-eighths to three-quarters square or half by one and a half-inch openings of sixteen-gauge steel wire or even heavier material is preferred. The wire needs to be heavy because the cage bottom must support the weight of the rabbit and possibly a bit of occasional thumping. The rabbit cannot escape, nor can small animals easily tear the wire and attack your pet. The heavy gauge also permits quick and efficient cleaning. Remove the rabbit so the cage can be hosed down and scrubbed with a stiff brush to loosen any stubborn debris. Sponge it down with a household disinfectant and then rinse it very thoroughly, because the cleaner is probably poisonous to your pet. A rabbit establishment that is well-designed and well-cared-for will be virtually odorless even on a hot summer day. After all, rabbits are not smelly; it is their old and stale excrement that is.

A rabbit can be housed in a cage, a simple enclosure with some reinforcement at the corners. Indoors, it is fine the way it is. However, if you plan to keep your animal outdoors, then a hutch is required. A hutch is a two-part enclosure consisting of the cage section attached to a weather-proofed section. Most rabbits are very hardy and can survive the coldest winters without heat, provided they have waterproof and draft-free quarters and dry bedding. Be sure that your rabbit can protect itself from sun, rain, cold winds, and freezing temperatures. The cage must be situated under a roof to block the elements. Or, you can build a structure similar to a tall table, but with a pitched roof to shed the rain. Storm curtains of canvas or plastic can be helpful, and in colder climates solid walls on the sides and back of this "table" are required.

The hutch should be easily transportable so your pet can travel. You can place the cage near you in the back yard or take it along on vacation. Simple movement of the hutch also facilitates cleaning.

# TROPICAL FISH HOBBYIST

Helping marine, freshwater, and herptile hobbyists, for 42 years

• January, 1994 •
$2.95/$3.95
(Canada & Foreign $4.50)

The Timbt Danio

Colorful Plants

ISSN 004-3269

**Let** *Tropical Fish Hobbyist* magazine show you how to enjoy the tropical fish hobby to the fullest. Open up a whole new fascinating world with your own personal subscription to the largest, oldest and most colorful aquarium and tropical fish magazine.

**YES!** Please enter my subscription to *Tropical Fish Hobbyist*. I enclose payment for the length I've selected. U.S. funds only.

☐ 1 year—$30.00    ☐ 2 years—$55.00    ☐ 3 years –$75.00    ☐ 5 years—$120.00
12 BIG ISSUES     24 ISSUES     36 ISSUES     60 ISSUES

Canada, add $11.00 per year; Foreign add $16.00 per year. Please allow 4-6 weeks for your subscription to start.

| Prices subject to change without notice. |

☐ SAMPLE ISSUE—$3.50 ☐ LIFETIME MEMBERSHIP $495.00 (maximum 30 years)

☐ GIFT SUBSCRIPTION. Please send a card announcing this gift. I would like the card to read:

SEND TO:
Name _____

Street _____ Apt. No. _____

City _____ State _____ Zip _____

CHARGE my: ☐ VISA ☐ MASTER CHARGE ☐ PAYMENT ENCLOSED

_____
Card Number

(Minimum order charge $15)

Cardholder's Name (if different from "Send to:")
_____

Cardholder's Address (if different from "Send to:")
_____

_____
Cardholder's Signature

View from above of the interior of an outdoor rabbit hutch. The baffle allows the occupant of the hutch to escape the effect of cold winds and provides additional security.

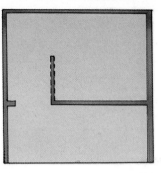

IMMEDIATELY ABOVE:
This outdoor housing unit is set within an enclosure protected by a low fence, which provides at least minimal security. Features of the structure include a set-back entrance, which allows the provision of a "front porch" effect; elevation of the base of the unit above the ground; and a slope to the rear of the roof, facilitating rain run-off.

AT RIGHT is a partial view of indoor temporary housing quarters that would be less suitable for rabbits than good-quality metal cages.

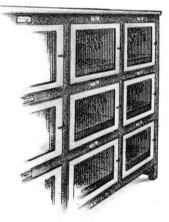

If left outdoors, the hutch needs to be protected from predators. A sturdy fence not only prevents a rabbit from escaping, it also keeps other unwanted animals, thieves, and children out. A hutch at eye level affords additional protection and is good for the rabbit keeper because problems are easy to see and correct without bending down or reaching up.

An all-steel cage is easily sterilized, will not get smelly, cannot be chewed, and will ultimately last longer and cost less than other types. If for some reason a wooden cage is chosen, all wooden parts exposed to the rabbit should be covered with wire mesh to minimize the ravages of gnawing.

Buy your first cage or hutch from a pet shop. Professionals have probably recognized and overcome problems that you never thought of, and they can probably construct the cages with less expense. After you have had some experience, you may elect to improve on or modify the structures. However, adhere to the basic designs and use materials which have proven effective over time.

## ACCESSORIES

Metal cages do have some drawbacks of which you should be aware. First, if the cage is outdoors in a cold climate, the metal will get cold quickly and draw body heat away from your pet. Placing a wooden board in the cage for the animal to rest on can prevent chilling. Second, if your rabbit is a thumper it may get sore hocks from hammering the wire floor. Again, a wooden board in the cage may relieve or prevent this discomfort.

In winter, you may want to spread hay on the cage floor to provide additional warmth. Remember, though, that it will need to be changed regularly. If you would like to do even more, a box about a foot by a foot and a half in size can be placed in the cage and a hole cut in the side for the rabbit to enter and exit. Drill holes in the bottom for drainage and pro-

FACING PAGE:

This sturdy metal cage has been equipped with carrying handles to make its transport easier, and it also contains a metal partition to separate animals as required.

Your pet's cage should be lightweight, durable, and easy to clean. Photo courtesy Rolf C. Hagen Corp.

vide fresh bedding material. Keep the box and the bedding dry to prevent colds and chills from the dampness.

In warm weather, a rabbit should be shaded from the direct rays of the sun. If the temperature soars to about 90°F, place a jug of frozen water in the cage before your pet gets wet around the nose and mouth. A plastic milk container works well. Your rabbit will lie beside the jug and the ice will keep it cool. Having two jugs allows you to replace the melted one immediately.

You may wonder what your rabbit will do all day when you are not giving it attention. Much of the time will be spent eating and nibbling, or just lying around. However, providing a few toys will be a welcome diversion. A stick or a branch from a tree, particularly fruit trees, that can be chewed and gnawed is great fun. Be sure to wash off the dirt and avoid those trees where insecticides have been sprayed. Small containers, like empty frozen juice cans, can be tossed and rolled around. Be creative, being careful of objects that may be poisonous or have small pieces that can break off and choke your pet. A Nylabone chew product (the 'petite' size) is the ideal chew. It is hardy and easy to sterilize. Purchase it at any pet shop.

## ROAMING LOOSE

You may decide that you would like to let your rabbit roam loose inside the house or out in the yard. Your pet must be trained enough, however, to let you pick it up whenever you want to retrieve it. Otherwise, you may never catch it. Allow your rabbit to get used to your handling in a confined area, a small room or the fenced-in area around the hutch, where you can easily catch it. Repeat letting the animal loose and picking it up so it does not run from your advances.

If you let a rabbit loose in the house, remember that these animals are avid chewers. Constant supervision is needed so that the rabbit does not destroy furniture or gnaw electrical cords. Some rabbits can even be paper-trained or kitty-box-trained, but this requires a great deal of patience and persistence on your part. Also, do not bring your pet in from the cold to play and then put it back outside. Sudden and extreme changes of temperature can lead to illness. Better to leave the rabbit outdoors altogether because it can withstand very cold temperatures without ever being brought inside.

There are many kinds of good bedding materials from which you can choose. Photo courtesy Rolf C. Hagen Corp.

37

Rabbits that are permitted to run free in the yard should be fenced in or carefully trained to stay within the confines of a specific area. It is still best to have a fence, because even if your pet won't run away, it may be attacked by other animals or thoughtless children.

Some plants, such as rhododendrons, are poisonous to a rabbit. Since a rabbit will nibble on the grass, be sure that your lawn has not been treated with insecticides or chemicals which may be lethal. You are responsible for knowing your yard and making it safe for your pet.

In picking up the rabbit, support must be given to the body much as it is here, with the weight resting mostly on the lifter's hand. Additional support is provided by the hand cradling the shoulders. Under no circumstances can the rabbit be left to dangle unsupported, as permanent damage could result; additionally, a rabbit treated badly during one episode of handling can become averse to being picked up in the future.

## HANDLING

Never lift a rabbit by the ears! A rabbit's ears are delicate and easily injured. A rabbit needs to be lifted in such a manner as to make it feel comfortable and secure. A frightened rabbit may bite, kick, scratch and struggle to get away. Unfortunately, many rabbits are harmed or killed due to mishandling.

A tame rabbit responds well to gentle human companionship. Often, bunnies will sit in your lap content to be stroked and snuggled. To properly lift the rabbit, one hand should grasp the loose skin across the shoulders or the chest. The animal should be held with its head up and the belly

against your chest. One hand now supports the back of the neck and the other hand is under the rump, carrying most of the weight. Or, the rabbit can be cradled much as you would a baby. The belly is up, with the head high and the tail low.

Wearing a long-sleeved shirt of sturdy material protects you from the sharp toenails of a rabbit. Keep in mind that your clothing may become soiled from "accidents," and may pick up some rabbit fur. Therefore, do not wear clothing that you prefer to keep in top condition.

Ear tattoos are very useful as permanent markings that provide positive identification and leave no doubt as to a rabbit's ownership.

## IDENTIFICATION

If you plan to keep more than one pet, you might want to record some vital information on a card hung outside each cage. With large numbers of rabbits, it's amazing how easily you can become confused, because rabbits can look pretty much the same. You should keep a written record of the rabbit's name or number, birth date, weight, and parents. Also, mark down when the animal is mated, who was the partner, and notes about the offspring. This helps you to single out good breeders and discontinue the mating of poor specimens. The breeders will not be over-age, and new breeders can be chosen on the merits of their breeding history, as well as displaying desirable features.

Permanent markings consist of a metal leg ring on a hind leg or a tattoo in the ear. The identification numbers are assigned by the breeders' association that you join and are kept in their records.

Rabbits are rather hardy animals, and with clean housing, a proper diet, and plenty of water, they should live out their lives relatively free of disease. Preventive maintenance is the most important aspect in controlling infections and vermin infestation.

# AILMENTS

Check your pet every day. Look for bright, alert eyes and a glossy sheen to the coat. Be sure it is eating well and is active. The droppings should be large, round and firm. If you note any changes in the rabbit's habits or health, be prepared to take it to a veterinarian.

If you already have one or more rabbits, quarantine any new specimens before introducing them to the herd. The newly acquired rabbits need to be at least 100 feet away, or in another room if possible, for at least a month. Any signs of illness can be spotted before it is passed on to other rabbits and throughout the colony.

Some common health problems are listed below.

### Molt

Rabbits first molt between the sixth and fifteenth weeks of life. Thereafter, a rabbit will molt yearly, probably in late summer or autumn. This is a normal occurrence and should not be mistaken for the shedding caused by ticks or fur disease. Add about one-half teaspoon of cod liver or linseed oil to the diet to help replace natural oils.

### Diarrhea

Sometimes associated with another illness, diarrhea can be the result of too many greens in the diet. Withhold the greens and water, and administer kaopectate. The dosage is determined by the weight of your rabbit.

### Coccidiosis

This is the most common infection among domestic

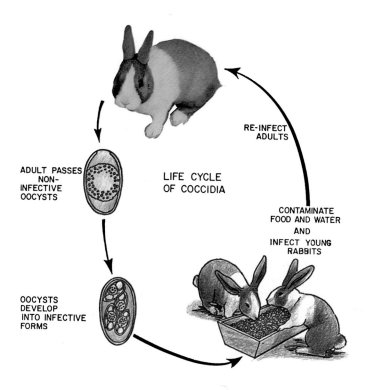

ADULT PASSES
NON-
INFECTIVE
OOCYSTS

LIFE CYCLE
OF COCCIDIA

RE-INFECT
ADULTS

CONTAMINATE
FOOD AND WATER
AND
INFECT YOUNG
RABBITS

OOCYSTS
DEVELOP
INTO INFECTIVE
FORMS

The above is a schematic representation of the life cycle of the protozoan parasites that cause coccidiosis in rabbits.

rabbits. It is caused by a protozoan that affects the liver. Your
pet will appear listless and have a lack of gloss and general
roughness to the fur. It will also exhibit a loss of appetite, yet
be pot-bellied and have diarrhea. Sulfaquinoxaline sodium con-
trols the parasite. Follow the directions on the bottle which is
available in pet shops and local feed and grain stores. Some rabbit fanciers use the medication on a regular basis to control
coccidiosis.

**Toenails**

Toenails grow constantly and are quite sharp since
they are used for digging and fighting. If your rabbit's nails are
particularly long or twisted, trim them with a tool available
from your pet dealer or with diagonal pliers. Clip a little at a
time to avoid severing the blood vessel that extends into the
base of each nail.

**Teeth**

The incisor teeth grow continuously and are worn down by the food a rabbit eats. It is unusual for them to become overgrown. However, if they need to be clipped, see a veterinarian. If the incisors grow too long, the animal cannot eat and will starve to death.

**Sore hocks**

If your rabbit has pain on walking or the feet become ulcerated, it has sore hocks. This is typically the result of thumping on hard or rough cage bottoms or infections associated with unsanitary conditions. Wash the infected areas with

Although rabbits are not rodents, they share with rodents the characteristic of having incisors that grow continuously; the feeding of hard foods such as rabbit pellets helps to keep the teeth from growing too long.

soap and water, then dress with antibiotic ointment. Be sure the cage is always clean and dry, and give the rabbit a board to sit on to get its feet off the floor.

**Ear mites**

Ear mites are indicated by crusty scabs in the ears that occur from a rabbit's constant scratching. A stiff neck and eye muscle spasms are also symptoms. To drown the mites and loosen the scales, apply about a half a teaspoonful of mineral

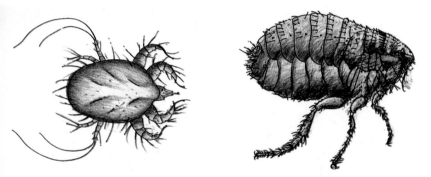

Mite (left) and flea—typical of the type of parasites that attack small mammals such as rabbits, dogs, etc.

oil in the ear with an eye dropper. Repeat this several times. Or, you may prefer to use a medication recommended by your veterinarian.

**Snuffles**

The cause of snuffles is crowded, dirty housing. Your pet will have sore-looking eyes, a runny nose, and sneezing. The hair on the front feet will become matted from wiping the nasal discharge. The treatment is, of course, to correct the housing and to treat the animal with an antihistamine.

**Mucoid enteritis**

Most common in rabbits five to eight weeks of age, the

symptoms of this disease are listlessness, jelly-like feces, excessive thirst, fever, and overall scruffiness. The stomach is full of water. The rabbit so afflicted needs to be treated by a veterinarian.

### Heat stroke

Due to excess exposure to the direct rays of the sun, an animal suffering from heat stroke will lie quietly on its side and breathe heavily. The best prevention is to provide a shaded, well-ventilated area in the outdoor hutch. Provide plenty of cool drinking water and periodically dampen the hutch with water. Placing a jug of ice in the cage helps to keep the rabbit cool.

For a rabbit suffering from heat exhaustion, wrap it in cool, moist towels. Do not immerse your pet in cold water or it may go into shock.

An open cage such as this one housing a beautiful Tan rabbit is easy to clean and very secure, but it does not provide any shade on a hot day unless some type of covering is placed over it.

FACING PAGE: Medicating the ear of a rabbit. Be extremely careful when administering any type of medication so that no harm is done to the pet.

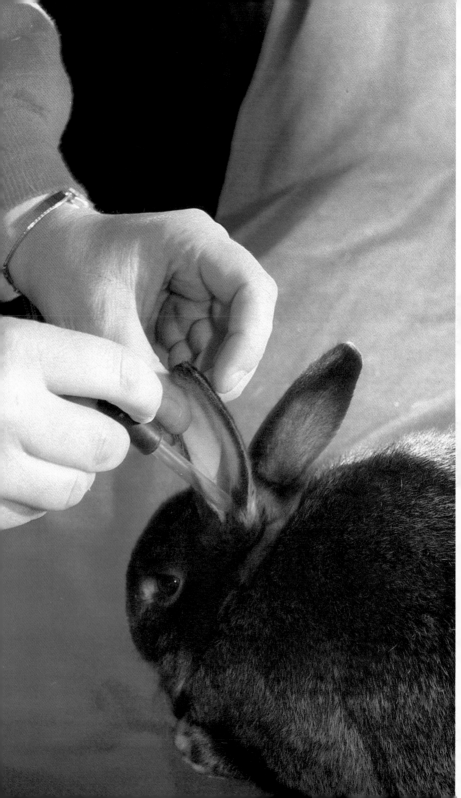

## Eye infections

More common in baby rabbits, the eye and eyelids will be inflamed with pus under the lids. Apply antibiotic ointment and keep the bunny out of cold drafts.

## Blue breast or mastitis

A doe will have a swollen milk gland which may be tender and appear dark. This is a bacterial infection that follows a physical injury. Prevent injury to the mammary glands by protecting the animal from all sharp edges in the cage. Check for nails and protruding end wires. Smooth the edge of the nest box. Clean and disinfect the hutch.

## Pneumonia

A bacterial or viral infection, pneumonia occurs more frequently in does that have been dampened or chilled. A rabbit will breathe rapidly, have a nasal discharge, and hold its head high. This infection is in advanced stages once *you* are able to diagnose it. Contact your veterinarian.

## Ringworm

Circular areas of hair loss and scaly, red inflamed skin indicate ringworm, caused by a fungus; infected animals should be dipped in a lime-sulphur solution.

## Euthanasia

Old rabbits may become stiff, slow, pained, and more subject to illness. It is in the rabbit's best interest to euthanize it quickly and painlessly, rather than to let it suffer. The thousands of rabbits sold for meat are treated in the same humane manner you could use for your pet.

Your veterinarian can give the aged or sick rabbit a shot that will calmly put it to sleep and let it die painlessly and quickly with no trauma.

Mini lops are the smallest of the lop rabbits but have the same great appeal as their larger cousins.

**Black Netherland dwarf rabbit.**

*Above:* Sable point Netherland dwarf rabbit. *Below:* Blue Netherland dwarf rabbit.

The best diet for a captive rabbit is actually a very simple one. Animal nutritionists have developed a pelletized rabbit food containing all the calories, vitamins, minerals, fiber, fats, and proteins, in a scientific ratio, that rabbits need. The pellets are a blend of alfalfa or clover hay, cereal grains, and minerals. Check the label. The protein content should range from 12-15% for dry does, bucks, and developing young. For pregnant does and mothers of nursing young, the percent should range from 16-20%. Commercial rabbit pellets, purchased from any pet shop, are a safe, convenient, completely nutritious, and inexpensive diet. Everything a rabbit requires to grow and reproduce is contained in each single unit.

# NUTRITION

How much your rabbit eats a day will depend on the size and age of your pet. A five-pound rabbit will consume approximately five ounces of dry food daily. You should give your pet all the pellets it will eat. To find out how much that is, simply provide your rabbit with a few ounces of pellets. If some pellets are left uneaten, give less the following day. If the bunny seems ravenous when you come around the next day, leave a little more. By knowing how much food your rabbit eats it is easy to monitor its food intake. Any changes you note may indicate that something is wrong.

FACING PAGE:
Cartoons and other popular entertainment media have associated carrots with rabbits, but a steady diet of rabbit pellets is much better for pet rabbits than fresh greenfoods of any kind.

The pellets should be provided in a feed crock or a feed hopper, both available in pet shops. The dish should be strong, rust-resistant, and tip-proof. A dish that tips easily wastes food, and one that is easily nibbled does not make a good dessert. Or you may prefer to use a hopper feeder. This device mounts on the outside of the cage, which allows you to feed your rabbit without opening the door. A hopper permits

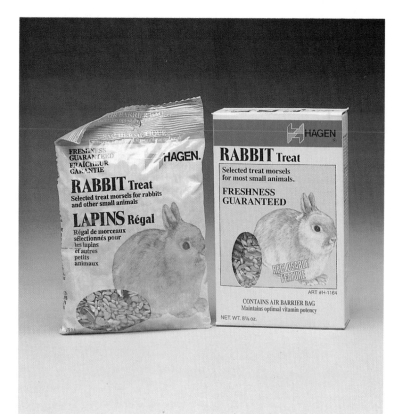

Pet shops stock a variety of food items for rabbits, including treats. Photo courtesy Rolf C. Hagen Corp.

you to put in extra pellets if you plan to be away for a day or two. Be sure to locate the dispenser where it cannot become wet or soiled. Wet or damp pellets will disintegrate or get moldy. If your pet eats this food, it will surely become ill and may die. By no means let any uneaten pellets remain in the dish to get stale. Replace all the pellets with fresh food every day.

Buy a few weeks' supply of rabbit pellets at a time so it remains fresh. Stale food will lose its nutritional value. The pellets need to be stored in moisture proof containers in a cool, dry place. Keep it out of the sun and out of reach of mice, rats, and other rodents. To remain a good food, the pellets should be clean, dry, fresh, and vermin free. Pellets kept in this manner will have all the dietary essentials maintained in their correct proportions.

No matter what breed of rabbit you have and no matter what type of solid food you feed it, a pet rabbit must always have access to a supply of clean fresh water. Pet shops sell a number of devices that make it easy to supply the rabbit with water without spillage.

As a supplement to the pellet diet, you may give your pet all the hay it wants. Alfalfa, or any dry, leafy, fine-stemmed hay will do. Some shops even sell alfalfa hay cubes that you can try.

An occasional fresh vegetable can be offered as a treat. Rabbits are known to enjoy carrots, sweet potatoes, turnips, apples, and cabbage. Fresh green grass and lawn clippings are acceptable, provided they have not been treated with herbicides or insecticides. Introduce any new foods slowly, and only one at a time. Sudden changes in the diet can play havoc with a rabbit's digestive system, and too many greens result in diarrhea. Never allow any rabbits under five or six months of age to feed on greens. Any fresh greens in their diet are too drastic a change for them at this young age.

Never offer your pet any greens that are not fresh enough for you yourself to eat. Do not leave the fresh food in the cage overnight because it may be spoiled by morning. Wilted, rotten foods can be dangerous to your rabbit.

An inexpensive way to have a constantly fresh variety of greens available for your pet is to make arrangements with your local grocer to pick up his fruit and vegetable scraps. He will probably be happy to let you have them knowing they are for your bunny. Your local baker is a good source of stale but **not** moldy bread. Rabbits enjoy nibbling on this tidbit.

Because rabbits eat dry food, a supply of cool, fresh water must always be available. A four pound rabbit will drink about one pint of water each day. A heavy bowl should be used, one that cannot be tipped over, and it should be rust and chew-proof. One quart of water should be provided every day; one pint for drinking, and the other pint for wasting. Remember that a rabbit may upset the dish, dribble the water on its fur and on the floor, dump food, shed hair, and soil the water. The water also attracts insects and in low temperatures will freeze. Ice is no substitute for fresh water. A rabbit needs water in liquid form. You may want to keep two water crocks so that as one freezes it can be replaced with a fresh one. Keep in mind that a nursing doe requires even more water because she is drinking for her babies as well.

## Nutrition

A better choice for watering equipment is a plastic or glass watering bottle with a stainless steel stem. Since it is hung outside the cage, it doesn't take up any room on the cage floor. The water stays clean because it is sealed up, and a rabbit cannot spill the water as it licks drops from the tube. The water bottle works well in warm weather, but it cannot be used when the temperature drops below freezing. A watering crock or dish must be used during this time.

Any receptacle that is going to hold food for rabbits should be heavy and easy to clean, and it should be kept free of chips and cracks that could harbor germs.

Before you begin to breed rabbits, a few things must be decided. First, each rabbit needs its own cage. Baby rabbits remain with their mother only up to three months. After that, do you have the space, time and money to keep several rabbits, each in its own cage? Second, if you do not intend to keep the rabbits,

# BREEDING

where are they going to go? Make arrangements to dispose of the rabbits either with friends or pet shops. Third, deciding what to do with the animals means that you have to produce a breed that someone else wants. Pet rabbits can really be any variety or combination. But for meat production a larger breed is preferred.

Depending upon the breed, rabbits mature sexually at various ages. Small breeds are ready at five months, the medium breeds at six months, and the giants at nine months. Does bred too early are more likely to resorb the embryos, abort, or produce stillborns.

Be sure the pair you decide to breed actually consists of a buck and a doe. (Yes, mistakes have been made). Keep them separated for a couple of weeks and observe them. Are they eating well and in top condition for mating? If all seems well, they can be brought together at any time because female rabbits do not have specific periods of time when they are fertile. They will allow mating to take place, and then several hours later the eggs will be fertilized.

Bucks will perform better on their own turf, so move the doe into his hutch. If you put him into her cage, fighting may break out. Do not leave them alone because if mating is going to occur it will be over in no time. The buck will mount the doe, she will lift her hindquarters, and almost immediately the act will be over. Don't be alarmed if the male suddenly falls over on his back or side. He will soon recover.

Return the doe to her cage and for the next week or so feed her the normal ration. After all, you can't be sure that

Pelleted food formulated especially for rabbits is the most important part of a rabbit's diet. It can be purchased in variously sized packages to meet the needs of the individual rabbit owner. Photo courtesy Rolf C. Hagen Corp.

she is pregnant, and if she isn't, you don't want to overfeed her. A fat doe may have difficulty getting pregnant or have complications giving birth.

On the twenty-seventh day after mating, a nest box and nesting material should be provided in the cage. All-wire nest boxes can be bought or wooden ones can be simply made. Average sized rabbits will make do with a floor space of twelve by eighteen inches. The box can be scaled up or down depending upon the size of the breed. One side should have an opening cut out for the doe to get in and out, or the entire side can be cut down to about six inches. The top of the box should be open, and the bottom needs a few holes for drainage. Straw, hay, or wood shavings make a good bedding material. The doe will then pull out fur from her own chest and stomach to further ready the nest.

Shortly before giving birth, the doe may go off her feed and her droppings may become large and soft.

If all goes well, about thirty-one days after mating the young will arrive. They are blind, naked, and really don't resemble rabbits much at all. While the female is kindling, she should not be disturbed. However, the day after the litter arrives the babies need to be checked. There may be anywhere from one to twelve pups, with the average litter being five or six. Any dead babies should be removed and you may choose to cull any obvious runts. Many breeders let them remain with the mother and let nature take its course.

When you examine the nest, the doe should be given some edible treat to occupy her time, then the box needs to be taken from her sight. Rub your hands in the cage litter before touching the babies so your human smell won't disturb the

Here the mother munches contentedly while her babies sleep. Note the white fluff surrounding the babies; it is fur from the mother's body.

mother when you replace her young.

If a doe you thought of as being pregnant does not give birth, suspect that she has been stressed by fear, rough handling, lack of food, or a chill. Early on in the pregnancy she may have resorbed her young, and it can be traced to a situation where you were at fault. She may be mated again, but be sure you correct any adverse situations. Keep her warm, well fed and in a safe and quiet area.

Leave the doe alone with her babies as much as possible. She will do all that is required to raise them correctly, keeping them warm and feeding them regularly. The nest box must be clean and dry and the doe provided with all she can eat and drink. Bits of greens can still be offered, and diluted milk is an acceptable dietary supplement.

In about ten days, the babies' eyes will open and their bodies will be plump and furred. By three weeks they will be scampering around the cage floor. At this time, discontinue the greenstuffs to be sure the young do not get hold of it. Such a drastic change in diet at this young age could be lethal. Not until they are six months of age should they be allowed food other than pellets and water.

The babies will begin to eat the pellets, but they are still nursing, also. Not until they are completely weaned should they be separated from their mother. This is usually between six and eight weeks of age.

Some breeders believe that it is best to remove the doe from the litter rather than the litter from the doe. This way the young can adjust to being without their mother before being introduced to unfamiliar surroundings. However, others prefer to remove the babies a few at a time to let the mother's milk gradually dry up. The larger babies are removed first while the smaller ones stay for more milk.

Although a doe may produce several litters each year, for her to remain in top form she should be limited to three. Let her rest for a minimum of three weeks after the young are weaned. If she is not in prime condition by then, allow some more time. The average breeding life of a doe is three years; up to five for a buck.

## SEXING

The litter needs to be separated soon after weaning to avoid fighting and unexpected mating. Before the young are fully furred, the sexes are easy to distinguish because the females have white spots on their bellies; these are the teats. Later on, though, sexing becomes more difficult.

Two people should be available to sex the rabbits. One restrains the animal while the other examines the genitals. The rabbit is held belly up with the hind legs spread apart. The second person applies slight pressure to either side of the vent. Males exhibit a penis that protrudes from a rounded opening. Females have a large, slit-shaped opening in about the same area.

With practice, one person will be able to roll a rabbit on its back, hold one hind leg in each hand, and use the thumbs to gently manipulate the area and expose the sex organ.

## HAND REARING

Occasionally, because of illness or death of the mother, pups need to be hand raised. This demands great time and patience, but these young are better pets because they lose their fear of humans.

The babies should be fed commercial baby milk at three-hour intervals. The mixture is prepared at about one and a half times the strength for human babies because rabbit milk is highly concentrated in comparison. The milk can be fed from an eye dropper, a toy doll feeding bottle with a rubber nipple, or a nursing bottle found in pet shops.

These young rabbits will develop at about the same rate as those reared by their mothers. At three weeks of age they should be taught to eat rabbit pellets and to drink water from a dish. The bottle feedings are gradually phased out.

## PEDIGREES

A standard is a written physical description of what characteristics a breed should exhibit. A purebred rabbit is bred to meet the requirements of an established and recognized breed, and all of its immediate ancestors are of that same breed.

## Breeding

A mongrel, or crossbreed, is of unknown ancestry. The rabbit may look like none you've ever seen before, clearly a mixture of two or more breeds. Or, there may exist no written history of the animal.

### CLUBS AND SHOWS

To really become involved in raising rabbits, you should join a club and enter your pet in rabbit shows. You'll learn a lot about rabbits, meet people who share a common interest, and have great fun. In the United States and England alone there are about 3,000 shows yearly. Throughout these countries there are local and national clubs, fairs, and pet shows that feature rabbits.

To obtain more information about memberships and shows, ask the pet dealer from whom you bought your rabbit.

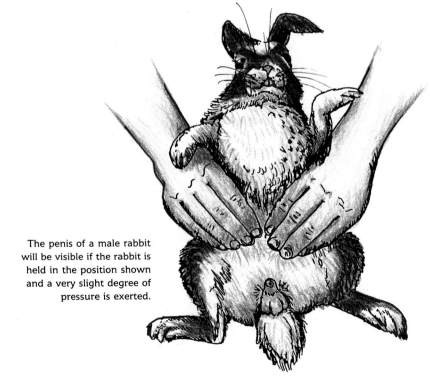

The penis of a male rabbit will be visible if the rabbit is held in the position shown and a very slight degree of pressure is exerted.

The following books by T.F.H Publications are available at pet shops and book stores everywhere.

## ENCYCLOPEDIA OF PET RABBITS—
**By D. Robinson**
**ISBN 0-87666-911-9;**
**T.F.H. H-984**

This is the most comprehensive, descriptive, and thorough text available on rabbits. Every aspect of successful rabbit husbandry is covered

# SUGGESTED READING

in detail. In addition, almost all of the recognized breeds, and many of the color varieties within each breed, are represented in full-color photographs.

*Hard cover, 5½ x 8", 320 pages. 231 full-color photos, 52 black and white photos.*

## STARTING RIGHT WITH RABBITS—By Mervin F. Roberts
**ISBN 0-87666-814-7; TFH PS-796**

This excellent book for beginners concentrates on the basics.

*Hard cover, 5½ x 8", 128 pages, 78 full-color photos, 10 black and white photos.*

## THE T.F.H. BOOK OF PET RABBITS—By Bob Bennett
**ISBN 0-87666-815-5; T.F.H. HP-014**

This book, written by the author of the Boy Scout manual about rabbit raising, is full of down-to-earth advice and rabbit lore. For those thinking of purchasing a pet rabbit, there is no better place to begin than the *T.F.H. Book of Pet Rabbits,* which will start the new owner out *right!*

*Hard cover, 8½ x 11", 80 pages, 85 full-color photos.*

## LOP RABBITS AS PETS—By Sandy Crook
**ISBN 0-86622-181-6; TFH PS-809**

The perfect book for anyone interested in any of the different breeds of Lop rabbit and how to care for them, written by a Lop enthusiast/breeder whose long experience is distilled into com-

pletely practical advice—and plenty of it.
*Hard cover, 5½ x 8"; 128 pages. Illustrated with many full-color and black and white photos.*

### DWARF RABBITS—By Gunter Flauaus
### ISBN 0-86622-180-8; TFH H-1073
This book is the introductory text for owners (and potential owners) of rabbits that have been bred down to smaller size than most of the breeds commonly available as pets; fine value for beginners
*Hard cover, 5½ x 8"; 128 pages. Illustrated with full-color and black and white photos.*

### ALL ABOUT RABBITS—By Howard Hirschhorn
### ISBN 0-87666-760-4; T.F.H. M-543
Contents: What About Rabbits? Rabbit Housing. Shipment of Rabbits. Feeding. Health. Breeding. Rabbit Handling. Rabbit Clubs. Standards And Shows. Profitable Commercial Aspects Of Raising Animals.
*Hard cover, 5½ x 8"; 96 pages. 32 color photos, 39 black and white photos.*

### A COMPLETE INTRODUCTION TO RABBITS—By Al David
### ISBN 0-86622-271-5 (Hardcover)
### ISBN 0-86622-28-2 (Softcover); T.F.H. CO-022
Great four-color artwork and photos combine with a practical and easy-to-read text to make a book of pure enchantment for beginning rabbit fanciers.
*128 pages, 5½ x 8"; almost 100 full color photos and drawings.*

### RABBITS—By Paul Paradise
### ISBN 0-87666-924-0; KW-021
This 96-page hardcover book is chock full of good advice and good photos; covers what a beginner really needs to know.

# Index